This or That Pets

Is a DOG or a CAT the Pet for Me?

by Jaclyn Jaycox

PEBBLE
a capstone imprint

Published by Pebble, an imprint of Capstone
1710 Roe Crest Drive, North Mankato, Minnesota 56003
capstonepub.com

Library of Congress Cataloging-in-Publication Data is available on the Library of Congress website.
ISBN: 9780756578879 (hardcover)
ISBN: 9780756578824 (paperback)
ISBN: 9780756578831 (ebook PDF)

Summary: Purr. Woof! Both dogs and cats are great furry friends! Compare these two popular pets side by side. Which needs more exercise? Which pet stays cleaner? Does one cost more? Then decide which one might make the best pet for you!

Image Credits
Capstone Studio: Karon Dubke, 8, 9, 11; Getty Images: LeManna, 7; Shutterstock: Africa Studio, 21, ANURAK PONGPATIMET, 13 (top), DimaBerlin, 13 (bottom), Giovanna Rim, 16, Gladskikh Tatiana, 15, Kati Finell, 14, Konstantin Aksenov, Cover (bottom), M. Schuppich, 20, Maria Moroz, 17, maroke, 6, MaszaS, 5, Natasha Pankina, background (throughout), New Africa, 4, Nina Buday, 19, otsphoto, 10, pattarawat, Cover (top), RossHelen, 18

Editorial Credits
Editor: Carrie Sheely; Designer: Bobbie Nuytten; Media Researcher: Jo Miller; Production Specialist: Whitney Schaefer

Printed and bound in China. PO 5834

Table of Contents

Words in **bold** are in the glossary.

Getting a New Pet

Wagging tails and soft purrs. Dogs and cats are popular pets! In the United States, about 65 million homes have dogs. More than 46 million families own cats. Let's find out which one might be better for you!

my PET
FOOD
PET

Exercise

Just like people, animals need exercise to stay healthy. Dogs should have 30 minutes to two hours of exercise every day. At least two walks a day is best.

Cats need about 30 minutes of exercise a day. But cats can't play as long as dogs. You can break up their exercise into shorter play sessions.

Cuddly or Not

Do you want a pet you can cuddle with? Dogs and cats can both be great snuggle buddies. Cats are more **independent**. But they often enjoy being petted.

Each cat or dog is different. Some enjoy being close to their owners. Others like their space. Many dogs and cats don't like to be picked up and held. But they may cuddle next to you.

Quiet or Loud

Woof! Dogs can be noisy! Dogs may bark or howl. They might whine and **whimper**.

Cats make noises too. But they are much quieter than dogs. Cats meow. They might be hungry or want attention. Cats also purr. They often do this when they are happy or **content**.

Clean or Messy

Cats **groom** themselves. They don't need baths. Dogs don't clean themselves well. Owners need to give them baths. Cats and dogs need to be brushed regularly to keep their coats healthy.

Dogs poop and pee outside. Owners clean up after them. Cats use **litter boxes**. Litter boxes should be cleaned every day.

Cheap or Costly

Some **breeds** of dogs and cats can be very **expensive**. The cost to buy a dog is usually higher than a cat.

Both dogs and cats need good care. They need to go to a **veterinarian** at least once a year. Dogs and cats need shots to keep them healthy. They need food to eat. Pets should have toys to play with too. Cats usually cost less to care for than dogs.

Handling and Training

It's important to be careful with your pet. Handle them gently. Cats can scratch or bite if you play too roughly. Dogs can bite if they are scared. It's important to **socialize** them. This helps them get used to different surroundings, people, and other animals.

Dogs can be trained to learn many commands and tricks. Cats can be trained too. But dogs are easier to train than cats.

Short or Long Lives

Getting a new pet is exciting! But remember that they can be part of your family for many years. Many dogs live 12 years or more. Cats live around 15 years.

Dogs and cats are great furry friends! Which would fit best with your family?

Which Pet Is Best for You?

Dogs and cats both make wonderful pets. This activity can help you figure out which one might be right for you.

What You Need:

- 2 cups
- marker
- marbles, coins, or other small items

What You Do:

1. Take two cups and set them in front of you. Use the marker to label one for dog and the other for cat.
2. Gather marbles, coins, or other small items.
3. Consider different questions. Are you an active person? Would you enjoy walking a dog or playing fetch with it every day? Or are you more relaxed? Consider what space a cat or dog might need. Do you have room for a large pet? Or would a smaller animal fit better in your home? As you go through these questions, place one of your items in the cup that best matches your answers.
4. When you are finished, see which cup is fuller. You might have found which pet is best for you!

Glossary

breed (BREED)—a certain kind of animal within an animal group

content (kuhn-TENT)—to be happy and satisfied

expensive (ik-SPEN-siv)—very costly

groom (GROOM)—to keep clean

independent (in-di-PEN-duhnt)—wanting to be free to do what one chooses

litter box (LIT-ur BOX)—a container indoors for a pet to go to the bathroom

socialize (SOH-shuh-lize)—to train to get along with animals and people

whimper (WIM-pur)—to make soft crying noises

veterinarian (vet-ur-uh-NER-ee-uhn)—a doctor trained to take care of animals

Read More

Gaertner, Meg. *I Like Cats*. Mendota Heights, MN: Little Blue House, 2020.

Jaycox, Jaclyn. *Read All About Dogs*. North Mankato, MN: Capstone, 2021.

Perl, Erica S. *Truth or Lie: Cats!* New York: Random House, 2021.

Internet Sites

Active Wild: Dog Facts for Kids
activewild.com/facts-about-dogs-for-kids

The Cat Fanciers' Association: About Cats
cfa.org/kids

National Geographic Kids: 10 Awesome Dog Facts!
natgeokids.com/uk/discover/animals/general-animals/dog-facts

PetMD: 10 Fun Facts About Cats
petmd.com/cat/general-health/fun-facts-about-cats

Index

About the Author

Jaclyn Jaycox is a children's book author and editor. When she's not writing, she loves reading and spending time with her family. She lives in southern Minnesota with her husband, two kids, and a spunky goldendoodle.